Introduction

Under the cover of the Second World War the Nazis tried to kill every Jewish person in Europe.
For the first time, science and technology were used not to improve people's lives but for the mass murder of a whole people. Six million Jews, including 1,500,000 children, were murdered: this is called the Holocaust. The Nazis also enslaved and murdered millions of other people because of racism, intolerance and prejudice. Roma and Sinti people (sometimes called Gypsies), people with disabilities, Poles, Soviet prisoners of war, Jehovah's Witnesses, homosexuals and others were killed in vast numbers.

None of this happened very long ago: some of the people involved are still alive today. Nor did it happen very far from where you live. These events occurred in the 'civilised' countries of modern Europe. So it was not only the lives of people at the time that were torn apart by the Holocaust but also our ideas about how human beings treat each other. Because of this the Holocaust is important not only as an event in history but also for how we live our lives today.

Of the nine million Jews alive in Europe before the Holocaust, six million were murdered. Of the nine people in this photograph, six were murdered. The only survivors were two men (in the centre and on the right) and the youngest boy.

In these photographs we glimpse a world that no longer exists: they show the lives of Jewish people, both rich and poor, living peacefully in Europe before the Holocaust.

Many religious Jews wanted to hold on to the customs and traditions that had preserved Jewish life for centuries. For these people it was important to honour God in everything they did. Rules about how to behave towards each other had been written in their holy books thousands of years earlier and were still used as a guide for how to live a good life.

Most Jews who still followed a very traditional way of life lived in shtetls, small towns and villages in Eastern Europe where the majority of the inhabitants were Jewish. Many lived in great poverty, but their wealthier Jewish neighbours provided help for those in greatest need.

Millions of Jews in Eastern Europe spoke Yiddish as their first language, but the language of study and of the synagogue was the ancient language of their ancestors: Hebrew.

The Yiddish-language film advertised on this film programme reflects how Jews in Eastern Europe could often lead very different lives: look closely and you will see scenes of both traditional and modern life, the old and the new, existing side by side.

The Bund was a Jewish socialist organisation that campaigned to improve the lives of the Jewish working class in Poland. Social clubs, welfare organisations, newspapers, theatres and music all helped to maintain a Yiddish-speaking Jewish community quite separate from the much larger non-Jewish society.

Many Jews no longer lived separately from non-Jews, particularly in the countries of Western Europe where they dressed in the same way as their non-Jewish neighbours, lived and worked alongside them, and spoke their language. The majority still kept important Jewish holy days but, for many, religion was no longer the most important part of their lives.

Zionists in Germany preparing for a new life in Palestine. Zionists believed the only way for Jews to live free from persecution was to go to Palestine and rebuild a Jewish homeland.

As you can see, Jews all over Europe often led very different lives. They lived in different countries, had different political beliefs and spoke different languages; some were rich while others were poor; there were Jewish doctors and lawyers, Jewish factory workers and Jewish businessmen, Jewish farmers, builders, carpenters and tradesmen, shop owners, market stall traders, scientists, artists and musicians. All were individuals with different personalities, hopes and ideas about how best to lead a happy life.

But, whatever their differences, the Jews of Europe also shared many things in common – with each other and with their non-Jewish neighbours.

Like people everywhere, they fell in love, married and had children.

*Those who could afford to went on **holidays**, and many more enjoyed simple days out with their friends.*

4

Many joined sports clubs. This photograph shows the members of a Jewish football team from Eastern Europe.

Education was important to Jewish families, whether that meant sending their children to a Jewish school like this one in Eastern Europe...

...or to the same school as the children of their non-Jewish neighbours.

Why were Jews hated?

The Nazis were racists. They thought German people belonged to a 'master race' that they called 'Aryans'. The Nazis hated black people, Gypsies, and Slavic people from Eastern Europe, but most of all they hated Jews. Hatred of Jewish people is called antisemitism.

Look closely at this antisemitic drawing published by the Nazis in a children's picture book.

- How has the artist tried to make the 'Jewish' man appear?

- Does this drawing actually look like the Jewish people whose photographs you have already seen?

- Why do you think that antisemites used drawings rather than photographs of real people?

- How must it have felt to be an ordinary Jewish person living at this time, with such images appearing in books and newspapers all over Europe?

6

Test these Nazi claims with the historical evidence:

Claim **The Nazis said that Jews were a threat to Germany and that they were trying to destroy the 'German way of life'.**

Fact Less than 1% of the total population of Germany were Jewish. Could they really have been a threat to the 'German way of life'?

Claim **The Nazis claimed that Jews gave nothing to German society.**

Fact Most German Jews came from families that had lived in Germany for hundreds of years. They thought of themselves as Germans first, and as Jews second. They were proud of the German culture and way of life. The Nobel Prize is awarded to men and women for outstanding achievements in the Arts and Sciences. By the end of the 1920s, Germany had won more Nobel Prizes than any other country; more than half of these German prize winners were Jewish. Does this show a people who contributed nothing to German society?

Claim **The Nazis blamed Jews for Germany's defeat in the First World War.**

Fact During the First World War 95,000 Jewish soldiers served in the German Army; 35,000 were awarded medals for bravery; 12,000 died fighting for Germany. Does this show a people who wanted Germany to lose the war?

Claim **The Nazis said that Jews were Communists who wanted to spread the Revolution that had happened in Russia in 1917 to other European countries, including Germany.**

Fact The majority of German Jews were middle class, professional people, such as doctors, lawyers and businessmen. Communism was a working class movement that would seize the property of the middle and upper classes. Is it likely that many German Jews supported the Communists?

So why did the Nazis blame the Jews for all of Germany's problems?

For nearly 2,000 years, Jews lived as a small minority in every country in which they made their home. As a minority they were treated with suspicion simply because they were 'different' and were often blamed for things they hadn't done. Christians falsely blamed Jews for the murder of Jesus and centuries of persecution followed. Thousands of Jews were burned to death for 'causing' the Black Death in the Middle Ages. When a Christian child disappeared, Jews were sometimes accused of murdering them and innocent people were punished. The Nazis continued this long tradition of 'scapegoating' the Jews: blaming them for any problem that they couldn't easily explain.

Racists don't see people as individuals. To the Nazis, all Jews were the same: lazy, selfish, untrustworthy, dangerous. Of course, most didn't even know any Jewish people because their hatred stopped them from spending time with Jews. They didn't know how ordinary Jews lived because they never visited their homes and families; they didn't know what Jews thought and felt because they didn't have any Jewish friends. They simply believed the lies that had been told about Jews for centuries.

Adolf Hitler led the Nazis to power in 1933 promising to make Germany powerful and respected by the rest of the world. He promised to fight Communism, to find jobs for the six million unemployed workers in Germany, to restore law and order, and to get rid of the 'Jewish influence' in Germany.

Hitler's speeches were full of hatred for the Jews and this encouraged his followers to attack Jewish people. The Nazis controlled the police and the law courts, and Jews soon discovered that they would have no protection against the Nazi attacks.

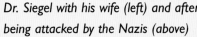

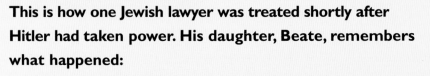

The Siegel family

Dr. Siegel with his wife (left) and after being attacked by the Nazis (above)

Beate Siegel

This is how one Jewish lawyer was treated shortly after Hitler had taken power. His daughter, Beate, remembers what happened:

On 10 March 1933 my father went to the police headquarters to lay a complaint on behalf of one of his clients who had been arrested. When he got to the police headquarters someone said to him, 'Dr. Siegel you're wanted in room number so-and-so' – which happened to be in the basement – and my father said, 'Fine, I'm in good time, I'll go there first.'

And when he got there he saw that it was full of Brown Shirt thugs who proceeded to beat him up. They knocked his teeth in and bust his eardrums. They then cut off his trouser legs and took off his shoes and socks, and hung a placard around his neck with the legend, 'I am a Jew and I will never complain to the police again.' They led my father around Munich in that condition for maybe an hour, and then they let him go.

We do not know whether Hitler planned to murder the Jews when he first took power. At first the Nazi persecution was intended to force Jews out of their jobs and to make life so unpleasant for them that they would leave Germany to live in other countries.

Jews were forbidden to be lawyers, teachers and dentists, members of the civil service, journalists, vets, or doctors. They were forced out of jobs in the theatre and banned from the German armed forces. Jews were not allowed to be members of German sports clubs or social clubs. Signs were put up in restaurants and parks and on the outskirts of towns saying 'Jews not wanted'.

In 1935 a law was passed that Jews were no longer citizens of Germany: even if their families had lived in Germany for generations, they were now classed as 'foreigners'. Jews were no longer allowed to marry 'Aryans'. Jews who had sex with an 'Aryan' would be sent to prison. A year later Jews were no longer allowed to own bicycles, typewriters or records.

In March 1938 Germany united with Austria and 190,000 Austrian Jews soon became victims of Nazi persecution.

In 1938 all Jews had to have their passports stamped with the letter 'J' to make them easy to identify.

The first concentration camps

The first concentration camps were set up to terrorise the Nazis' political opponents. Thousands of communists, socialists and leaders of trade unions were sent to the camps where they suffered hard labour, meagre rations, beatings and torture. Nazi Germany was ruled by terror. Anyone who spoke out against Hitler risked being sent to a concentration camp. Many thousands of homosexuals, Jehovah's Witnesses, Gypsies and Jews were also sent to these brutal camps.

Kristallnacht – the Night of Broken Glass

By 1938 many Nazis felt that Hitler had not done enough to drive Jews out of German life.
On 9 November 1938, as he sat at a dinner table in Munich, news reached Hitler that a Nazi shot by a young Jewish man a few days before had died in hospital. Hitler turned to Joseph Goebbels, seated beside him, and said quietly, *'The SA should be allowed to have a fling.'*

The SA (or 'storm troopers') were the Nazis' own private army. These few words from Hitler were the trigger for a night of violence in which nearly 100 Jews were murdered, synagogues all over Germany and Austria were burned, Jewish-owned shops and businesses were smashed up, and more than 20,000 Jewish men were sent to concentration camps.

Rudi's father and mother

Rudi Bamber

The Bambers' café

Rudi Bamber

Eighteen year-old Rudi Bamber lived with his parents above their café in Nuremberg. You can see them here in photographs taken during the 1930s. Rudi recalls what happened to them on the night of 9 November 1938, while the family slept in their beds:

Late at night the front door was smashed in and a group of brown-shirted SA storm troopers marched in and began to smash things up, furniture, crockery, in the first floor of the restaurant. We were upstairs and were afraid to deal with this.

Then in the early hours, about one or two o'clock in the morning, another group came in. They came upstairs and started to attack my father and myself. They took me downstairs into the basement and began to beat me up.

I was taken outside. They had smashed everything they could possibly find, slashed paintings, furniture,

smashed a few water pipes so water was pouring out. And there I stood outside in the early hours of a November morning, just dressed in pyjamas and a dressing gown, under guard, waiting to be taken away.

They gave me a kick to go inside. I went through the house, it was a picture of absolute chaos, the floor was littered with broken glass and crockery and pieces of furniture thrown about, and the stairs were difficult to walk on because the pictures had all been smashed and everything had been thrown about. I came upstairs where my parents and grandparents were and I found my father lying on the ground on the floor there, not moving. And obviously he was dead.

I was very upset. I couldn't bear it. I tried to give him artificial respiration but of course it was no use. My mother was weeping – there wasn't anything more that could be done.

For the Jews, the world seemed to be divided into two parts - those places where they could not live, and those where they could not enter.

Chaim Weizmann

In the early years of Nazi rule many Jews chose to stay in Germany, believing that conditions would eventually improve. Most of those who tried to leave found safety abroad in Britain, Europe, the United States and Palestine, which was then under British control.

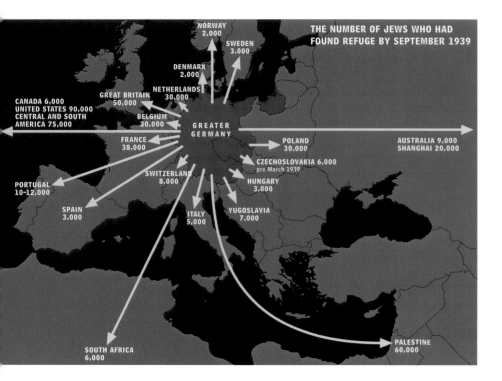

THE NUMBER OF JEWS WHO HAD FOUND REFUGE BY SEPTEMBER 1939

NORWAY 2,000
SWEDEN 3,000
DENMARK 2,000
NETHERLANDS 30,000
GREAT BRITAIN 50,000
CANADA 6,000
UNITED STATES 90,000
CENTRAL AND SOUTH AMERICA 75,000
BELGIUM 30,000
GREATER GERMANY
FRANCE 38,000
POLAND 30,000
AUSTRALIA 9,000
SHANGHAI 20,000
CZECHOSLOVAKIA 6,000 pre March 1939
SWITZERLAND 8,000
HUNGARY 3,000
PORTUGAL 10-12,000
SPAIN 3,000
ITALY 5,000
YUGOSLAVIA 7,000
PALESTINE 60,000
SOUTH AFRICA 6,000

Later, as Nazi persecution reached new heights, Jews became increasingly desperate to emigrate but found that the rest of the world was unwilling to help them all. After Germany united with Austria in 1938, and with the invasion of Czechoslovakia in 1939, the number of Jews trying to escape increased dramatically.

Hundreds of thousands found themselves trapped in Nazi-controlled lands. The Nazis would not allow Jews to take money with them and other countries would not accept large numbers of penniless refugees, especially at a time of worldwide unemployment. While most were appalled by the Nazi persecution of the Jews, widespread antisemitism also made people reluctant to welcome Jews into their own countries and strict limits were placed on the numbers of refugees they would help.

In 1939 the *St Louis* sailed to Cuba carrying 930 Jewish refugees from Nazi Germany but, when it arrived, the Cuban authorities turned the ship away. The *St Louis* then sailed along the south coast of the United States but the American government would not allow it to land either. It seemed that the Jews on board, having come so close to safety, would now be forced to return to Nazi Germany. Britain, France, the Netherlands and Belgium eventually agreed to divide the refugees between them. However, those who didn't land in Britain found themselves again under Nazi rule when Germany conquered Western Europe a year later. Most of the passengers aboard the *St Louis* did not survive the war.

A Kindertransport train leaves German (above) and (right) a new arrival in Brita

In 1917 Britain promised the Jews that Palestine, then under British control, would once again become their 'national home'. This caused anger among the Arab population of Palestine who saw the land they had lived in for thousands of years as rightfully theirs. As Hitler's demands in Europe threatened war, Britain became anxious to protect her position in the Middle East and the supplies of oil that would be vital to her armed forces. In 1939 Britain limited Jewish entry to Palestine in order to keep peace with the Arabs. In doing so Britain denied the Jews a place of safety when they needed it most.

- Do you think that Britain and other countries should have accepted more Jewish refugees from Nazi Germany?

- Should Britain help people seeking asylum from persecution today?

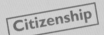

Daily Mirror cartoon of 6 June 1939

The *Kindertransport*

Our first day in Birmingham was hell. It suddenly hit me that we were in a foreign country without knowing the language, without relatives or friends, and I was trying desperately to be brave as a thirteen year-old boy was expected to behave. I spent most of that day in and out of the toilet so that no one could see the tears rolling down my cheeks.

Herbert Holzinger

Shocked by the violence of *Kristallnacht*, Britain did agree to take in 10,000 Jewish children in 1939. Parents were then faced with the agonising choice of sending their children away to a foreign country or keeping the family together. Eventually 9,354 Jewish children arrived in Britain under the *Kindertransport* scheme. Most never saw their parents again.

Desperate people queued for hours for the papers that would give them permission to enter a safe country.

Frank Foley

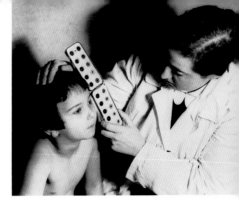

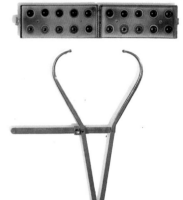

Frank Foley

Frank Foley worked for the British Government in Berlin. He had to decide who would be given permission to travel from Germany to Britain and its Empire.

Foley was so horrified by the Nazi treatment of the Jews that he issued thousands more visas than he was allowed to. Most of the visas were for Palestine, despite strict British restrictions on emigration there. He also hid Jews in his home and even went into concentration camps to get them out, at great personal risk. Some 10,000 Jews are believed to have escaped Nazi persecution because of his actions.

Instruments used by Nazi race scientists to determine hair and eye colour and to make skull measurements.

The staff of the Hadamar asylum in 1942. Hadamar was one of the institutions where people with disabilities were murdered.

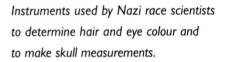

Today the British Government and others applaud the action of Frank Foley: a British man who saved thousands of Jews from the Holocaust. But at the time he was defying the British Government and breaking British law.

We often think of a 'good citizen' as someone who respects the law.

- Is it ever right to break the law?

- How far should someone obey laws that they believe to be wrong?

- Should we pick and choose the laws we want to follow?

- Was Frank Foley a 'good British citizen'?

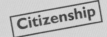

The racial state

'Race scientists' wrongly believed they could tell a person's character by the colour of their eyes and hair, the shape of their skull and the proportions of their features.

These ideas began in Britain in the nineteenth century and were popular in the USA and Europe by the 1920s. The Nazis were strongly influenced by these theories. They didn't believe human beings were equal but claimed there were superior and inferior 'races'. Germans were supposedly part of a master race called 'Aryans'. At the bottom of the Nazis' list of races were black people, Gypsies, Slavs and Jews. To the Nazis these people were not only 'inferior' to the Aryans, they were hardly human beings at all.

German Gypsies were registered, photographed and fingerprinted.

Sterilisation

The Nazis hoped to make Germany stronger by encouraging Aryan couples to have more children. At the same time they were afraid that children born to mixed-race couples would destroy the 'purity' of the Aryan race. Because of this, Gypsies and black people were sometimes operated on to prevent them from having children.

The Nazis also saw people with disabilities as a threat to the 'purity of the Aryan race' and thousands were sterilised to prevent them from having children.

My mother woke me at 6.30am. I said, 'What's happening?' She said, 'Come on, my boy, it's time to go to hospital.' The doctor was wearing an SA uniform. He made two cuts around my testicles. Sometimes I'm glad I couldn't have any children. At least they were spared the shame I lived with.

Thomas Holzhauser, a black victim of the Nazis' forced sterilisation programme

Euthanasia

The Nazis only valued the lives of people they thought would make Germany stronger. The care for people with disabilities was seen as a waste of money, so in October 1939 Hitler ordered their mass murder. More than 200,000 innocent people were killed by gas, starvation, and lethal injections in the 'euthanasia' programmes that followed. The doctors and policemen involved in this first large-scale killing programme were later transferred to Eastern Europe to apply their methods in the death camps of the Holocaust.

Dr. Ernst Gassen became depressed after losing his job for criticising the Nazis and was admitted to an asylum. He was gassed at Hartheim clinic in March 1941.

15

A young Polish girl grieves over the body of her sister, killed by German bombs during the Nazi invasion of Poland in September 1939.

Terror strikes Poland

I have placed my Death's-Head formations in readiness – for the present only in the East – with orders to send to death mercilessly and without compassion, men, women, and children of Polish descent and language. Only thus shall we gain the living space that we need.

Adolf Hitler, August 1939

On 1 September 1939 Hitler invaded Poland. Two days later Britain and France declared war on Nazi Germany and the Second World War began. The Soviet Union and the United States did not enter the war against Nazi Germany for two more years, when Hitler declared war on them.

Hitler's aim was not only to rule more land. This was to be a racial war. Hitler wanted to destroy the people who already lived in Eastern Europe to make room for members of the 'Aryan race'.

Poland was attacked by massive forces on three sides. Two weeks later, under a secret agreement between Germany and the Soviet Union, Poland was also invaded from the east by the Soviet army. Within weeks Poland had disappeared from the map of Europe, divided between Nazi Germany and the Communist Soviet Union. Both ruled with terror and killed Poles and Polish Jews in vast numbers.

In the Nazi-controlled areas, Poles were to become slaves for the 'Aryan race': German settlers and Polish families of German descent. Polish children would be given only the most basic education. Heinrich Himmler, the head of the SS, decided in 1940 that Polish education must stop after the fourth year of primary school:

'The sole goal of this schooling is to teach them simple arithmetic, nothing above the number 500, writing one's name and the doctrine that it is divine law to obey the Germans … I do not think that reading is desirable.'

To destroy Polish resistance the Nazis established 300 concentration camps and prisons and murdered teachers, priests and political leaders. Large numbers of Polish civilians were shot or hanged for breaking even the most trivial Nazi rules. About 1,800,000 non-Jewish Polish citizens were killed as a result of Nazi terror.

The Polish priest, Piotr Sosnowski, moments before he was shot by the Nazis

If the international Jewish financiers in and outside Europe should succeed in plunging the nations once more into a world war, then the result will not be ... the victory of Jewry, but the annihilation of the Jewish race in Europe!

Adolf Hitler, January 1939

Hitler saw the conflict as in part a war against the Jewish people. Although the Jews wanted only to live peacefully and had no nation or army of their own, Hitler really believed they were secretly plotting Germany's total destruction.

In the early years of the war there was not yet a plan to murder all the Jews of Europe. However, from the very beginning, the Nazis singled out Polish Jews for 'special treatment': measures that were harsher even than the brutality inflicted on the Poles.

Look closely at the faces of the people in this photograph.

Kitty Hart-Moxon

Kitty Hart-Moxon remember Jewish life under Nazi rule in the Polish city of Lublin:

Things changed for us almost instantly ... We had no means of supporting ourselves, all the banks had been seized by the Germans or all the accounts had been frozen ... Very soon decrees went up in the city ... We had to register, and of course once we did that they knew where everybody lived, where everybody was. You couldn't move from one part of the city to another, you had to re-register, or you had to have sort of an exit permit to go from one place to another ... It wasn't very long before all Jews had to wear the Star of David ... The decrees went up to announce that all Jews would have to move to a different part of the city.

All Jews over the age of 12 had to wear a white armband with a blue Star of David or sew a yellow star onto their clothing. Marked out in this way, Jews were in constant danger of attack.

Jewish communities were ordered to create Jewish Councils, which were made to carry out German orders – or decrees – under threat of death. Jews were forced to move into 'ghettos': areas of towns that were sealed off from the outside world with walls and fences. By mid-1941 nearly all of the Jewish population in German-occupied Poland had been imprisoned in these overcrowded slums. Many Jews were forced to work in labour camps under appalling conditions.

- Do they look as though they are 'only obeying orders', as many later claimed?

Kitty Hart-Moxon

And we didn't realise that this was the start of the ghettos.

But it was one incident that made Kitty really understand how serious their situation had become:

I was walking the street with a friend, a boy of my age. The decree was that when German soldiers walked on the pavements everybody else had to get off into the road. I stepped into the road but my friend didn't, and the soldier pulled out a gun and shot my friend through the head.

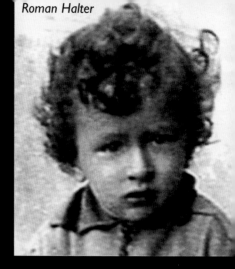

Roman Halter

Roman Halter was born to a very religious Jewish family in Poland, the youngest of seven children. Growing up in a loving home, Roman had a happy early childhood in the small market town where he lived.

The bustle of the market place would disappear every Shabbat as the Jewish community prepared for worship in their simple wooden synagogue. Every Friday night, the men of the town purified themselves in the hot waters of the ritual bath-house. Roman was always disappointed when his father – a timber merchant – would send him out of the changing rooms just when the men began to sing songs and tell rude jokes.

Roman's closest friend was Karl Eschner. Karl's family had moved to Poland from Germany some years before. The fact that Roman was a Jew and Karl a Christian made no difference to their friendship as they played football and volleyball together, and swam in the lake with the other children from their town.

When the Nazis invaded they ordered that Germans living in Poland should not mix with Jews. Soon Karl stopped playing with Roman and spent more and more time with the local Hitler Youth group that the Nazis had formed. One day Roman met this group as they were out training and they surrounded him in the street. The group leader ordered Karl Eschner to knock Roman down. Without argument Karl punched Roman hard in the face, knocking him to the ground where he lay for a moment, stunned.

Some time later, Roman was returning home from a nearby town when he heard the sound of gunfire. Moving quietly through the forest he came to the top of a ravine and peered into the valley below. Beneath him Roman saw Jews from his school being forced into the ravine by uniformed men. As he lay hidden from view he saw Karl Eschner and other young men from his town murder the Jewish neighbours they had once played with as children.

Hitler conquers Europe

In 1940 German forces swept through Denmark,
Norway, Luxembourg, Belgium, the Netherlands and
France. The British army was forced to retreat and a
desperate evacuation at Dunkirk ferried troops back
across the Channel to safety. With Hitler's total
victory almost complete, Italy joined forces with
Germany and invaded France, Albania and Greece.
In 1941 German and Hungarian troops invaded the
Balkans. By May 1941 Hitler dominated Europe from
France to Poland and from Norway to Greece.

Conditions under German occupation varied from country to country. Once again Nazi policy was decided along 'racial' lines with the most brutal treatment inflicted upon the 'Slavic' peoples of Eastern Europe and the Balkans.

In all countries under Nazi occupation the antisemitic laws passed in Germany during the 1930s were swiftly imposed. Jews were forced to register their names and addresses with the authorities; they were sacked from jobs in teaching, the civil service and other professions; Jewish businesses were taken over, Jewish property was confiscated and Jews were barred from using public services.

Everywhere the Nazis needed assistance from the local population to carry out its actions against the Jews. This collaboration was widespread: local police and officials carried out round-ups and deportations of Jews. In France foreign Jews were willingly handed over to the Nazis by the French authorities; Croatians and Romanians massacred large numbers of Jews and Gypsies; Bulgaria handed over Jews from the areas of Greece it had occupied but protected Bulgarian Jews; in the Channel Islands (which fell to the Nazis in 1940) the British population did little to protect the few Jews who had not fled to the mainland ahead of the Nazi occupation.

In 1941 Hitler invaded the Soviet Union. In some places the antisemitism of local people erupted into mob violence against their Jewish neighbours, even before the Nazis arrived.

Germany

Belgium

Netherlands

France

Slovakia

Hungary

From 1941 Jews in all Nazi occupied territories were forced to sew a yellow star onto their clothing.

21

A war of extermination

This struggle is one of ideologies and racial differences and will have to be conducted with unprecedented, unmerciful and unrelenting harshness.

Adolf Hitler, 1941

On 22 June 1941 Hitler invaded the Soviet Union. Three million Soviet soldiers were taken prisoner in the first eight months. Jews and those suspected of being Communists were shot immediately. The rest were imprisoned in camps and left to starve or freeze to death.

Hitler saw the Soviet Union as the heartland of his most hated racial and ideological enemies: Jews, Slavs and Communists. This was to be a racial war of extermination that would destroy entire communities. Nazi terror became organised mass murder.

Four SS murder squads, called *Einsatzgruppen*, followed the advancing German army, moving from village to village and shooting thousands of Jews, Communists and Gypsies into mass graves.

Although mass murder had begun this was not yet part of a plan to murder every Jewish person in Europe. Jews not killed by these death squads were packed into newly created ghettos, similar to those in occupied Poland, while their fate was decided. From October 1941 the Nazis began to deport Jews from the other occupied countries to the East, crowding them into the ghettos of Poland and the territories conquered from the Soviet Union.

Soviet POWs captured by the German army in the southern Ukraine

A Nazi murder squad near Dubossari in the southern Ukraine

SITES OF
EINSATZGRUPPEN KILL

LENINGRAD
- Murder sites
- Cities
- Nazi-dominated countrie
- Nazi-occupied Soviet terr
- Soviet territory

MOSCOW

EINSATZGRUPPE A

EINSATZGRUPPE B

WARSAW

EINSATZGRUPPE C

STALINGRA

EINSATZGRUPPE D

DUBOSSARI

BUCHAREST

22

Inside the ghettos

At first the Nazis didn't have a clear plan of what they would do with the millions of Jews who came under their control. The ghettos were established to control the Jewish population while a detailed plan was decided upon. Meanwhile, conditions inside the ghettos of Eastern Europe continued to deteriorate.

A soup kitchen inside the Warsaw ghetto

Warsaw ghetto

No one could leave or enter the ghettos without a special permit. The Nazis forced Jewish leaders to form councils to run the ghettos and to carry out their orders. Jews were given very little food – sometimes as little as 184 calories a day (about the same as a few slices of bread). Starvation became widespread.

We had a very tiny room in which we had two beds, a couch, a small round little table, two chairs, that's all. And there was an oven, which you ... see only in the Baltic States ... it was tiled, a big tiled oven and we couldn't walk amongst all these things because there was no room, it was just too crowded. In the front of this room we slept: my mother, myself, my sister on the couch, and a young girl from another house used to come in her pyjamas to sleep with my sister because she had no sleeping accommodation where her parents lived. In the kitchen on a dais a little bit higher with a curtain slept Mr. Katz – who was one of the leaders of the community in the ghetto – and opposite him, also behind a curtain, slept a couple from Austria.

Marsha Segall

Overcrowding rapidly became a major problem. *In Warsaw 30% of the city's population was forced into just 2.4% of its space. Conditions became worse as Jews from surrounding towns and then from other countries were also crammed inside the ghetto's walls. In such overcrowded and unsanitary conditions disease spread quickly.*

David Sierakowiak was fourteen when he was forced to move to the Lodz ghetto. He kept a diary of his experiences there.

24 May 1941
I've been catching up with classes all day today. I'm hungry as hell because there isn't even a trace left of the small loaf of bread that was supposed to feed me till Tuesday. I console myself that I'm not the only one in such a dire situation. When I get my bread ration I can hardly control myself, and sometimes I suffer so much from exhaustion that I have to eat whatever food I have, and then my small loaf of bread disappears before the next ration is issued, and my torture grows. But what can I do? There's no help. Our grave will apparently be here.

David died in the ghetto on 18 August 1943.

For some the conditions inside the ghettos were too much to bear and they committed suicide. For others, only their own survival counted and they would do anything to save themselves, even at the expense of other people. But many refused to have their spirits destroyed or to lose their human values. Some people kept diaries, determined to record the details of ghetto life. Others wrote poetry or painted pictures, and concerts were held within the ghettos. Illegal newspapers were printed and circulated. Community life continued and people supported each other: hospitals were established and soup kitchens helped those most in need.

Every able-bodied person was employed making things for German soldiers: producing uniforms, combat boots, metal parts for machinery. The people who were actually working would receive extra food rations. The elderly, the sick and the little children were hard pressed because they did not have those extra rations. So people were dying in the ghetto from sickness, starvation and lack of hope.

Marylou Ruhe

This photograph of Barbara Stimler with her mother and father was taken before the war

After Barbara's father was sent to a labour camp, she and her mother were moved into the Lodz ghetto. Here Barbara, still only a child, had to care for her sick mother. She begged for work in a children's hospital where she helped to care for children with tuberculosis, bathing the children, washing floors, and helping with the other duties.

Now if you didn't get work in the ghetto you didn't get a coupon to get soup and my mother did not get this soup because she was not working. Working in the hospital and explaining to them this situation they let me have soup to take home. On my day off I found a room for myself and my mother to have our own place. So it was like a little square room. We had two beds there … and two chairs and a little table, and that's where we lived.

Barbara's mother became more ill and she became paralysed on one side.

When I went to work I had to leave two chairs next to her, one with some food – whatever I had – and one with a bedpan. When I came back I had to clean her and look after her …

It was very, very difficult for me because I had to do everything for my mother. I had to stand in the queues for the rations sometimes until 11 o'clock in the night and carrying it all by myself on my shoulders. If it was a ration of wood or potatoes or coal it was very difficult for me because I did not have help from anybody … [It was] very difficult with my mother, seeing her going to nothing. On one leg she had little worms working on it, it was really pitiful, and all she needed was food.

One day they gave us a little ration of oil, a little bottle of oil. I didn't even touch it. Before I went to work I gave her a teaspoon every morning of this oil, thinking maybe that will help her. Nothing helped. She was just going to nothing …

Half a million Jews died inside the ghettos from starvation and disease. The only hope of survival was to obtain extra food smuggled illegally into the ghetto.

Parents could no longer protect their children or provide food for their families. Some smuggling routes were only accessible to children, and in many cases the children became the breadwinners of the family. Family relationships were turned upside down.

The place we used to go through was through some houses and cellars. I squeezed through a sewer and from the sewer over a wall and into a cemetery. From the cemetery we used to make our way into Warsaw proper, through a park.

Issy Rondell, a child smuggler in the Warsaw ghetto

Ruth Foster

Ruth Foster and her parents – the last photograph before they were deported to the Riga ghetto

Food being smuggled over the ghetto wall

Smuggling food was extremely dangerous. Ruth Foster's family were deported from Germany to the Riga ghetto in Latvia. Conditions there were very hard. Ruth remembers the food as, '*mainly consisting of frozen cod heads and frozen cabbage leaves and black bread.*'

Ruth's father was a member of a work party that was sent outside of the ghetto to saw wood. One day he, another man, and a young boy were caught bringing 'extra rations' into the ghetto.

The three of them were handcuffed and led to the market square where the other people from the ghetto were made to assemble.

Ruth and her mother were forced to watch as the German commander of the ghetto walked behind each of the three men. Ruth remembers: '*With his revolver he shot them dead. They fell dead in front of our eyes. That was the life of my father.*' They were killed for smuggling a piece of bread, a sandwich and a few potato peelings.

To have survived one day under those conditions and retain one's values was a great act of resistance.

Esther Brunstein

In spite of these conditions Jews struggled not only to survive but also to continue to live as normal a life as possible: to maintain their dignity and to hope for a better future.

Care for loved ones continued in the most difficult circumstances.

When religious services and rituals were banned they were continued in secret, sometimes in cellars and hidden rooms.

Although the future might have seemed hopeless, people still fell in love and got married.

To listen to a radio was punishable by death. Nonetheless, some people did take a few radios into the ghetto, and surreptitiously they listened to the BBC ... and somehow news got around, which gave us hope because it let us know that the outside world still existed.

Esther Brunstein

Schools were forbidden, there were no schools in the ghetto, but parents organised small groups of children, four or five at a time and of course there was no lack of teachers. We met once or twice a week because there was the death penalty for the children, the teachers, the parents and in fact everybody in the house if we were discovered ... There were not enough books and the books were out of date, they were pre-war, but we learned with great enthusiasm. People learned foreign languages, Latin, Greek, German, French, English. People were continuing with higher education, there were university professors who were also giving courses in everything.

Janina David

When Hitler came to power he wanted to drive Jews out of Germany. By 1940 he wanted to force Jews out of Europe. By 1942 death camps were being built in Poland to murder every Jewish person the Nazis could lay their hands on. How did blind hatred turn to planned extermination?

The 'Final Solution' of the Jewish Question – the organised murder of every Jew in Europe – was decided upon gradually and by stages, and only as other 'solutions' proved unworkable.

Until 1939 the Nazis tried to 'get rid of' Jews from Germany and Austria by making life so unbearable for them that they would move to other countries. However, while hundreds of thousands did leave Germany and Austria, Hitler's invasions brought millions more Jews under his control. Plans were then made to 'dump' all of Europe's Jews on the African island of Madagascar or deep inside the Soviet Union.

The decision for the 'Final Solution' appears to have been taken in late 1941. As the German forces failed to defeat the Soviet Union, German troops suffered heavy losses, and the spectacular German advance ground to a halt, plans to deport the Jews further and further east became impossible.

When the United States entered the war in December 1941 Nazi Germany faced the most powerful nation on earth. Germany was not prepared for a long war and Hitler's frustration now turned against the Jews of Europe, the people he always blamed for Germany's problems.

On 13 December 1941 – two days after Hitler declared war on the United States – Hitler's propaganda minister, Joseph Goebbels, noted in his diary:

'In respect of the Jewish question, the Führer has decided to make a clean sweep. The world war is here; the annihilation of the Jews must be the necessary result … If the German people have sacrificed 160,000 dead in the eastern campaign, so the authors of this bloody conflict will have to pay for it with their lives.'

Hitler had decided that no Jewish man, woman or child would remain alive in Europe.

SS plans for a crematorium and gas chamber, dated 27 January 1942

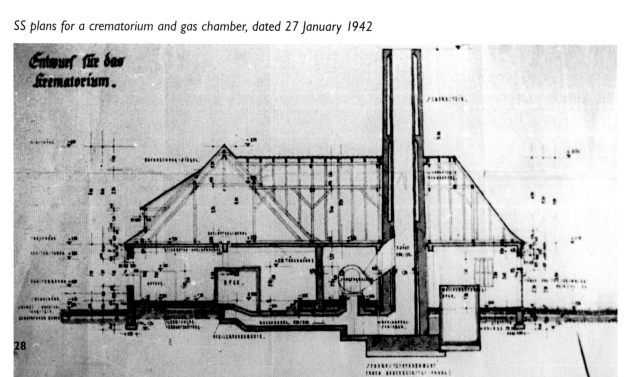

NAZI DEATH CAMPS

Tens of thousands of Jews could be killed in a few days by the SS murder squads. But the Nazis realised that shooting people into mass graves was too slow to be used for the murder of every Jew in Europe. They also wanted a method of killing that would cause less distress to the killers.

Scientists and engineers competed to find the fastest and cheapest way to kill people. The solution was found by building factories whose only purpose was the murder of human beings.

The first of these death camps opened in December 1941 at **Chelmno**. Gas vans were used to kill about 150,000 Jews, mostly from Lodz and the surrounding area, and several thousand Gypsies.

Three more death camps opened in the spring of 1942 near the villages of **Belzec**, **Sobibor** and **Treblinka** with the aim of killing all the Jews in occupied Poland. They used men and equipment from the 'Euthanasia' programme, and instead of gas vans they pumped carbon monoxide into gas chambers capable of killing more than a thousand people at a time. 1,600,000 Jews and thousands of Gypsies were murdered in these camps by the autumn of 1943. Gas chambers were built at **Auschwitz II-Birkenau** and **Majdanek** as the killing expanded to include all the Jews of Europe.

When all the Jews were inside the door was bolted. The driver then switched on the engine, crawled under the van and connected a pipe from the exhaust to the inside of the van. The exhaust fumes now poured into the inside of the truck so that the people inside were suffocated. After about ten minutes, when there were no further signs of life from the Jews, the van set off towards the camp in the wood where the bodies were then burnt ...

Theodor Malzmuller,
a member of the SS in Chelmno

Guards at the death camp at Chelmno (above) and beer bottles and a glass (left) recently excavated from the death site. Alcohol was freely available to the killers, both in the Einsatzgruppen and inside the death camps.

Zyklon B pellets turn to poisonous gas at room temperature. These pellets were poured into the gas chambers of Auschwitz II-Birkenau. Five to seven kilogrammes of pellets were enough to kill 1,500 people.

Deception

**The Nazis told the Jews they were to be 'resettled':
sent to work for the Nazis in the East. Millions of people
arrived at the death camps believing they were about to
begin this new life. Nothing could have prepared them
for the truth – that 'resettlement' actually meant death.**

*These are some of the possessions that people brought with them.
Look closely and you will see many things that you probably have
in your own home today.*

The deception continued
when the people arrived
at the death camps.
Sometimes music was playing at the
train station. Flowers were planted to make some camps look
more welcoming. The new arrivals were told they would be given
a shower and would then be taken to their new accommodation.
But the 'shower rooms' were really gas chambers.

One visitor to Belzec described the gas chambers in that death camp:
*In front of the building there were pots of geraniums and a sign saying
'Hackenholt Foundation', above which there was a Star of David. The
building was brightly and pleasantly painted so as not to suggest that
people would be killed here. From what I saw I do not believe that the
people who had just arrived had any idea of what would happen to them.*
SS-Lieutenant Colonel Wilhelm Pfannenstiel

As people were made to undress they were told to tie their
shoelaces together and to remember the number on their clothes-
pegs so that they could find their clothes again when they returned
from the showers. Then they were led into the gas chambers and
the sealed door was locked behind them.

*I installed showerheads in the gas chambers. The nozzles were not
connected to any water pipes; they would serve as camouflage for the
gas chamber. For the Jews who were gassed it would seem as if they
were being taken to baths and for disinfection.*
SS-Corporal Erich Fuchs, who helped to build
the gas chambers at Belzec, Sobibor and Treblinka II

*Possessions included many personal
items. Shown here are a lipstick, a
perfume bottle and other items.*

In the largest gas chambers of Auschwitz II-Birkenau two thousand
people could be killed at one time.

The order they gave was that parents should hand over all their children up to 18 years of age ... the cries from the mothers, 'Almighty God! Help us!' It's still ringing in my ears.

Rene Salt

Friends and families were separated as some were deported and others, for the time being, remained behind.

Although the Nazis promised that people were being sent to the East for work, people became suspicious as the old, the poor, the sick and children were taken first.

From March 1942 the Nazis began to send thousands of people from the ghettos to the death camps.

Small ghettos could be emptied of people in a day or two. Larger ones took weeks or months, and the Jewish councils and ghetto police were forced to help the Nazis. The Jewish councils had to draw up lists of fellow Jews to be deported and the Jewish police had to help with the round-ups that took these people to the waiting trains.

Ben Helfgott remembers a Jewish policeman who hid his parents to save them from deportation:
He was told very simply: 'Either you deliver your parents or else we are going to take your wife and your son and you. We are giving you twelve hours to make up your mind.' He came home, he discussed it with his wife, he went to see his parents. Of course his parents said, 'We are older people, give us up.' In the end he delivered his parents ... I've often wondered how did he feel? How did he live with himself? He knew that he was giving his parents up to certain death, yet what options did he have?

Esther Brunstein

As rumours spread that those who were deported were sent to their deaths, many tried to save themselves by hiding during round-ups. Esther Brunstein recalls:

We lived on the third floor of the building, which was the last floor. And above it there was a loft that could be reached by a stepladder ... all the neighbours who stayed behind on this third floor decided to go up in the loft. And we left the loft door open, sort of to look less suspicious with the ladder there.

But there was one young couple who had a little girl [called Eljunia]. I think she was about two, maybe three. And they left her in a big wicker basket, because she was asleep ... because they thought [there would be] less danger ... they thought if awoken she would cry. They piled things on top in the hope that ... the basket won't be detected, won't be searched.

And we were all up there, and I remember huddling close to my mother and being afraid to speak. I remember seeing my whole life in front of me and I think I was saying goodbye to my young life. And we heard shots. We heard screams outside.

We were in semi-darkness ... And then we heard them on the first floor, opening doors,

shutting doors. We heard people scream, we heard people cry. On the second floor, then on the third floor. And they were all people that we knew well. They were our neighbours, with whom we shared this sad existence. And we were quite sure our hour had come.

They came to the third floor and had one of the Jewish policemen with them ... And we were holding our breath praying, really praying for little Eljunia and her parents, but our prayers didn't get us anywhere. They went into their room and we heard a shoving and a kicking and then suddenly we heard cries. 'Mummy, mummy,' and it was little Eljunia. And there were the parents, those young parents with us, and they couldn't do anything ... we simply just had to beg them, hold them down, 'Don't scream, don't make a sound, or all of us will go.'

We even heard the Germans saying to the policeman, 'Go up those steps and see if anyone is up there.' We saw the man climb up the stairs. He looked, saw us in the dark, and said, 'No one is up there.'

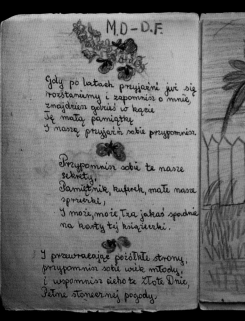 

Dosia's poem and drawing

Marysia

Until the Nazis marched into their town, Dosia and Marysia were inseparable. Then twelve-year-old Dosia, her parents and the other Jews in the town were forced into a ghetto and it seemed that the friendship would have to end. But Marysia, a Catholic girl, would slip into the ghetto from the 'Aryan' side to visit Dosia.

As the Nazis began to deport people from the ghetto, Dosia, her mother and a few others went into hiding in a secret attic. Marysia was one of the trusted few who knew where they were hidden and she continued to visit Dosia, at great risk to herself. Inside the attic Dosia and Marysia would whisper together, write poetry and draw. On 12 October 1942, while the girls were playing, the Nazis discovered the hiding place. Incredibly they allowed Marysia to go free but forced the Jews into the street at gunpoint, herded them to the station and onto the waiting train.

When after friendship lasting years
We part and you've forgotten me,
Somewhere in a corner
You'll find this little souvenir
And you'll remember we were friends.

You'll remember our special secrets,
The diary, the treasure box,
                        our angry little scraps,
And onto this book's pages
A tear will fall, perhaps, perhaps.

And as you turn each yellow page
You will recall when you were young
And recollect those golden days
So full of summer sun.

Written inside the ghetto
by Dosia Farbiarz
for her friend, Marysia.

Deportation

The Nazis were determined to murder every Jew in Europe. Trains from every country under Hitler's control were crowded with men, women and children. They rolled slowly across the continent to the death camps in occupied Poland. This final journey could take days, with the trucks so crowded that often there was not enough room to sit down.

The normal load for the trucks was sixty to ninety people; we were one hundred and twenty ... We had two buckets for our human needs. We had to overcome our inhibitions to use them – men, women, strangers, children – but we used them and they weren't quite sufficient for a hundred and twenty. With every jolt of the train the muck ran out, so we were sitting in it and we couldn't do a thing about it.

It was a very hot summer and there was very little air in the truck. The openings that we had – there were two openings – had barbed wire about three feet long and one and a half feet deep, these were the two openings where we got air for one hundred and twenty people and the air became really unbearable.

We were thirsty, we had a bottle of water to drink, most probably we drank it on the first day thinking that we could refill our bottles, but this didn't happen so we were getting thirstier and thirstier. We in our normal life talk about being thirsty, but thirsty there meant that one's lips were parched, broken, hurting, you were hungry, you had a piece of bread in your hand and you couldn't eat it because you couldn't swallow anymore.

It meant that people went into hysterics, people went mad, people had heart attacks and people died and we had the dead, the mad, the hysterical and the screaming amongst us and we could not do a thing about it.

Gertrud Levi

RAIL ROUTES USED FOR DEPORTATION 1941-1

Heading towards the unknown, some people managed to scribble notes to the loved ones they left behind. Throwing them from the deportation trains, they prayed that someone would be kind enough to send them on.

23 September 1942

My dearest little wife

The dice have been thrown. I am heading towards deportation and it is while the train is moving that I am throwing this last letter to an employee of the railways in the hope that he will post it without a stamp … I leave in good health and if we are able to resist the regime that is waiting for us, I will come back. I ask you to do as I am doing and to take courage and to hope. Don't renounce anything for yourself. Don't worry about your future, while you are waiting for my return. If I get out, I hope that we will live happily … Have confidence and don't fall into despair.

All my thoughts and all my love are in this last letter together with my gentle, tender kisses.

Your husband

Adrien

Adrien Cerf
The letter he wrote to his wife

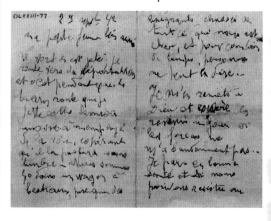

Adrien Cerf never saw his wife again. His train was destined for Auschwitz, where he was murdered.

Charles Van West was deported from Belgium to Auschwitz on 31 July 1944. He threw this letter from the train with a plea for whoever found it to post it on to Brussels. It contains his last words to his lover, Marie Legray, and a message for his sister, Mariette, and his parents who were in hiding.

In transport! I will return. The war is almost finished. Chérie, I will love you all my life!
Mariette and parents – you must be courageous.

Charly

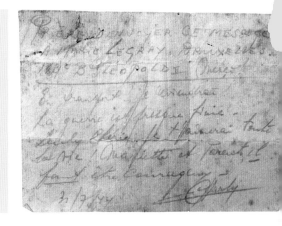

The screams from the mothers who were separated from their children, from the boys, their sons, from their husbands – it was just terrible.

Barbara Stimler

This group of women and children have been told that they are to go to the showers before being taken to a work camp. In fact it has been decided that these are people 'of no further use'. The SS doctor has sent them to the left, selecting them for immediate death. About 80% of the 1.1 million Jews to arrive at Auschwitz were sent straight to the gas chambers.

Long columns of those who had been chosen for the walk to the gas chambers struggled along the dusty roads, exhausted and in low spirits, mothers pushing prams, taking the older children by the hand.

Filip Müller

These women and children are waiting in a small birch grove outside one of the gas chambers. Inside, the group ahead of them has been led into changing rooms and told to undress for a shower. Once inside the 'shower room' the door is sealed and pellets of Zyklon B are poured into the room, releasing a poisonous gas. After about half an hour the chamber is opened and ventilated and Jewish slave labourers called Sonderkommando are sent inside to remove the bodies, extract any gold fillings they can find in the teeth of the dead, and burn the bodies in the crematory ovens. Shortly afterwards, this group of people will follow them.

Women and children were separated from the men and they were sitting in a small wood, which was just across from our barracks. Children would pick flowers, women would sit and picnic and give children some food and drink, which they brought with them ... Now the people sitting in the woods were totally calm. They had no idea that the people that had gone in front of them were already dead.

Kitty Hart-Moxon

Background photo: A model featured in the Exhibition depicting the selection of 2,000 Hungarian Jews from the Berehevo ghetto at the Auschwitz II-Birkenau death camp in May 1944.

Extermination by gas

Hungarian Jews arrive at Auschwitz in late May 1944.
They believe they are being 'resettled' and bring with them the belongings they need to start a new life. In the background you can see two buildings with large chimneys. These are the gas chambers and ovens of Crematorium II and Crematorium III. Within hours of this photograph being taken, most of the people you see here will have been murdered in the gas chambers and their bodies turned to ash in the crematory ovens.

Look closely at this photograph. This is the start of the 'selection'. Women and young children have been separated from men and older teenage boys. Leaving behind their belongings to be sorted by the prisoners wearing striped uniforms, these two groups will file past an SS doctor. He will send them to the left or the right. They will not realise that this simple gesture means the difference between life and death.

We stepped outside. We just didn't know where we were. There were all kinds of things happening. There were people in striped uniforms, shaven heads. It looked like an actual madhouse … And the people who were working there, we asked them, 'Where are we? Where are we?'
And they said, 'You don't know where you are?
You're in Auschwitz.'
'And what is Auschwitz? What's Auschwitz?'
'Well, you come here, but very few go out of here.' And they actually pointed to sort of smoke belching, chimneys. And said, 'That's what happens to people. That's what happens.'

Esther Brunstein

Auschwitz

As the train stopped we saw this time that flames were gushing out of a tall chimney into the black sky ... we looked at the flames in the darkness. There was an abominable odour floating in the air.

Elie Wiesel

*The smell of flesh being burned ... the air was not clean air:
you were breathing the dead really.*

Jan Hartman

37

Extermination through work

Auschwitz was both the largest of the Nazi killing centres and the largest of the concentration camps. Jews not selected for murder in the gas chambers on arrival were to be worked to death.

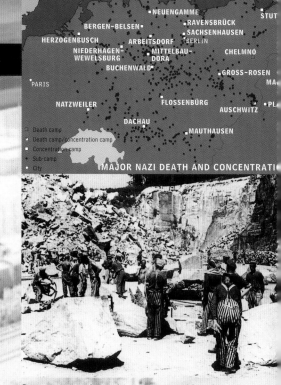

MAJOR NAZI DEATH AND CONCENTRATI...

More than two million men, women and children were forced to labour inside the vast system of Nazi concentration camps. As well as Jews they included political prisoners, Poles, Jehovah's Witnesses, homosexuals, Gypsies and others. Half were murdered or died from hunger, disease or overwork. A further four million Soviet prisoners of war were held in makeshift camps where three million of them starved or froze to death.

Prisoners work in the quarry at Mauthausen. The average life expectancy was three months.

Eating-bowl of Czech prisoner Prem Dobias. *Prisoners were given very little to eat – some watery soup or a piece of bread. Prem found nettles to add to his lukewarm soup to provide some essential vitamins. If a bowl was lost it could mean death, as without a bowl a prisoner didn't eat at all.*

The prisoners' day would start and end with roll call. At dawn each morning and again after they returned from work at night they were made to stand for hours, in all weathers, while the guards counted and recounted the living and the dead to ensure no one had escaped.

What is the value of a human life?

The SS carefully calculated how to make as much profit as possible from every human life. The possessions and clothes that prisoners brought with them were taken and sold. Prisoners' hair was cut off and sold for use as insulation in submarines and to make socks for submarine crews. German companies such as BMW, Siemens, Daimler-Benz, Krupp and Volkswagen paid the SS to use prisoners as slaves in their factories. Even after death the prisoners' bodies were used for further profit. Gold teeth were prised from the mouths of the dead, melted down and sent to Germany. The bones and ashes from their cremated bodies were sold as fertiliser. And money was made from the design of the killing process itself. Companies competed for contracts to build the gas chambers and the ovens in the crematoria, to make the sealed doors for the gas chambers and to supply the poison gas itself.

KOVNŌ
HOF
TREBLINKA
WARSAW
SOBIBOR
DANEK
BELZEC
ZOW

N CAMPS

I was with a mother and two daughters. When they came out with their hair shaved they didn't even recognise each other.

Tauba Biber

Everything was done to dehumanise the prisoners, to destroy each individual's identity. *All connections with prisoners' past lives were stripped away. On arrival their possessions were taken from them; their clothes were replaced with filthy uniforms which had belonged to those who had just died in the camp; their heads were shaved and they were classified and photographed. Prisoners were labelled with coloured triangular patches on their uniforms: black for Gypsies, red for political prisoners, pink for homosexuals, purple for Jehovah's Witnesses, yellow for Jews and so on. Even their names were taken from them: prisoners were given a number by which they would now be known. In Auschwitz this number was tattooed upon their left forearm.*

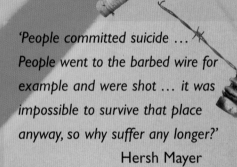

All day they worked at hard, meaningless labour, receiving terrible punishments for the most minor reasons. Prisoners were beaten and kicked, or attacked by vicious dogs.

Selections continued among the workers as SS doctors murdered prisoners deemed unfit for work. As a result prisoners who fell ill avoided the SS hospitals. At night prisoners slept for a few hours crowded together, usually in three-tiered bunks, in poorly heated, poorly ventilated barracks. In such conditions epidemics of diseases such as typhus and dysentery swept through the overcrowded barracks, killing thousands.

'People committed suicide ... People went to the barbed wire for example and were shot ... it was impossible to survive that place anyway, so why suffer any longer?'

Hersh Mayer

It seems unbelievable that companies would make money from such human misery. But even today there are companies whose search for profit blinds them to human suffering.

• Perhaps the trainers you wear were made in a sweatshop by workers in appalling conditions being paid poverty wages.

• Perhaps the chocolate you eat is made by a company whose policies cause malnutrition in developing countries.

• Perhaps the petrol in your parents' car was made by an oil company that invests in countries with appalling human rights records.

How responsible for this suffering are the people who work for these companies, and those of us who buy their products?

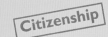

Citizenship

I don't remember seeing any heroic things because everybody realised as soon as one raised a hand against a German they would automatically take a hundred people ... and just shoot them.

Berek Obuchowski

Few people in Nazi-occupied Europe took part in armed resistance. Without weapons or military training and facing the threat of severe German reprisals most tried to live with the occupying forces as best they could. However, even faced with impossible odds, some Jews and others did fight back against the Nazis. Jews were active in partisan groups across occupied Europe, attacking German troops, blowing up bridges and train lines and committing acts of sabotage.

Jewish partisans fought the Nazis from the forests of Eastern Europe. This group of Jewish resistance fighters – called the Avengers – led attacks on the Germans in Lithuania.

Eva grew up in Budapest in a house that was filled with music. From a young age she dreamed of becoming a professional cellist, a musician like her mother. In 1944 Eva and her friend Klara were among the Jews deported from Hungary to Auschwitz II-Birkenau. Both Eva and Klara survived the selection made on their arrival and were sent to the concentration camps for slave labour. In Auschwitz and Ravensbrück they suffered a regime designed to destroy them physically and spiritually, surviving on starvation rations while being worked to the brink of death through forced labour.

Armed Jewish revolts took place in some 40 ghettos. The first and most famous occurred in the Warsaw ghetto where a desperate last stand of poorly armed Jews held out for four weeks against German soldiers armed with machine guns, tanks and flame-throwers. The Germans only defeated the resistance fighters after aircraft bombed the ghetto and soldiers burned it down, building by building.

Those who took part in uprisings knew they faced almost certain death, so such uprisings were usually in the final days of the liquidation of a ghetto, when all hope was slipping away.

Revolts even occurred in the death camps of Sobibor, Treblinka and Auschwitz where Jews seized weapons, killed their guards and set fire to crematoria and gas chambers. Escapes were made from camps and ghettos and thousands of Jews defied the Nazis by going into hiding.

Yet their friendship survived even these terrible conditions. On Eva's 21st birthday Klara gave her a tiny model of a cello, carved out of plastic stolen from the armaments factory in which they worked. It was to remind Eva of her childhood dream to become a musician and to give her hope that they might still have a future worth living for.

Resistance can take many forms. We have already seen the spiritual resistance of Jews who held on to their dignity, values and way of life amidst the starvation and disease of the ghettos and camps. Others resisted by recording the evidence of the Nazis' crimes, even at great risk to themselves.

In a speech to members of the SS in October 1943 Himmler said of the murder of the Jews, *'This is a page of glory in our history, which has never been written and is never to be written.'* The Nazis were determined that the evidence of their crimes would be destroyed so that the world would never know the true fate of Europe's Jews. When death camps were closed down the crematoria were blown up, the buildings demolished and trees were planted to hide the site of mass murder. As the Allied armies forced the Germans to retreat the Nazis burned documents to prevent the evidence of their crimes falling into Allied hands. They ordered prisoners to dig up and burn the bodies of thousands of their victims who lay buried in mass graves, and then killed these prisoners so that no witnesses would remain.

Resisting this were Jews who were determined that the world would know the truth and who risked their lives to preserve the evidence of these crimes.

This photograph was taken by members of the Jewish Sonderkommando *in Auschwitz II-Birkenau using a camera stolen from the SS. It was smuggled out of the camp by two political prisoners in September 1944 with a note that said,*

'We send you photographs from Birkenau – people who have been gassed. The photograph shows a heap of bodies piled outdoors. Bodies were burned outdoors when the crematorium could not keep pace with the number of bodies to be burned.'

The Sonderkommando *risked their lives to take this photograph so that the world would know what was happening to their fellow Jews, and so that you would know the truth.*

After the war milk cans and metal boxes were found buried under what was once the Jewish ghetto in Warsaw. On the eve of the destruction of the ghetto, documents detailing all aspects of Jewish life and suffering inside the ghetto were stored inside these containers and buried. The writers of these diaries, letters and articles knew that all hope of survival was lost, but were determined that the memory of life inside the ghetto and knowledge of the Nazis' crimes would not die with them.

Since the end of the war a number of documents written by members of the Jewish *Sonderkommando* have been discovered buried in the very ashes of Auschwitz. They detail the killing process. A note written by Zalmen Gradowski and hidden inside an aluminium flask reads:

Dear finder, search everywhere, in every inch of soil. Tens of documents are buried under it – mine and those of other persons – which will throw light on everything that was happening here. Great quantities of teeth are also buried here. It was we, the Sonderkommando, who expressly have strewn them all over the terrain, as many as we could, so that the world should find material traces of the millions of murdered people. We ourselves have lost hope of being able to live to see the moment of liberation.

In this final act of resistance those who preserved the evidence have been victorious. The fact that today we still learn about and discuss the Holocaust shows that the Nazis failed to hide their crimes and ensures the memory of their victims will never be forgotten.

I cannot write what I feel about this evil. My soul cries out in distress. I am a Jew, a Pole, a Greek, I am all women who are tortured, all children who are hurt, all men who die in agony.

A British woman wrote these words in her diary after hearing about the suffering of people under Nazi rule. She heard the news, believed what was happening and was tormented by her powerlessness to help. But for every person who reacted in this way there were many more who did not absorb the news of Nazi atrocities, or thought they were exaggerated, or whose own personal concerns overshadowed the tremendous suffering of those trapped under Nazi rule. A few even felt the Jews deserved their fate.

The British were able to understand secret German radio signals and knew about the actions of the SS murder squads in the Soviet Union as they happened. In 1942 news about the death camps reached Britain. Newspapers reported the murder of the Jews accurately. In 1944 eyewitness reports by escapees from Auschwitz reached Britain.

Campaigners, including the Archbishops of Canterbury and York and Member of Parliament Eleanor Rathbone, urged the Government to rescue the Jews. The majority of British people sympathised with the Jews of Europe, but few took part in campaigns to save them. Most were more concerned with how the war affected them, and with fears for the safety of their loved ones serving in the armed forces.

The British Government's priority was to win the war and they refused to use men, money and equipment for any other aim. It was believed that the best way of helping the Jews and others who suffered in Hitler's Europe was to defeat Nazi Germany. But, for the Jews facing total destruction, the end of the war would come too late. The tragedy was that the Nazis were far more determined to murder Jews than Britain and the United States were to save them.

Jan Karski

This sin will haunt humanity to the end of time.

Jan Karski

In December 1942, Polish courier Jan Karski came to Britain with detailed messages about the destruction of the Polish Jews. He met Foreign Secretary Anthony Eden, then travelled to the United States where he saw President Roosevelt. He toured the US giving public lectures that were well reported in local newspapers. Articles and a book that he wrote were published in America and Britain. But other than a statement by the Allied Governments that they condemned the Nazi murder of the Jews and a promise that they would put those responsible on trial, little was done to save the Jews.

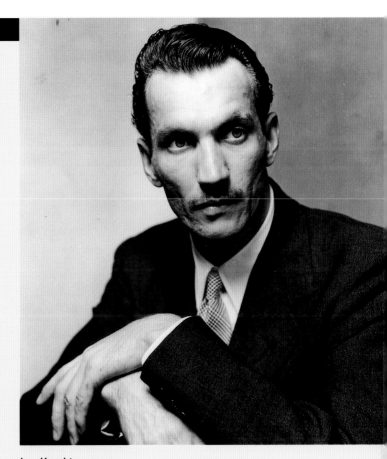

Jan Karski

Many years after the war Karski condemned those who claimed they didn't know what was happening to the Jews, those who said that the murder of six million Jews had been kept a secret. And he attacked not only those who committed the crime but also those who failed to prevent it.

Two hundred years before the Holocaust, Edmund Burke said, *'For evil to triumph it is only necessary for good men to do nothing.'* There are many tragedies in the world today that we feel powerless to prevent. But if we don't speak out against such things, who will?

Citizenship

45

In the continent ... you've got like a cellar underneath the house where you keep your potatoes during the winter ... In the cellar we dug out a hole [a metre long by a metre wide] and we moved into this hole. We put straw underneath ... and in this hole we were sitting ... I remember the first three days we were crying bitterly after our parents ... In this hole we were living for about seven to eight months in complete darkness.

Nathan Adams, who hid with his friend Julian
in the home of Polish Catholic Maria Cekalska

The punishments for helping Jews included imprisonment, torture and death. Most people were not prepared to risk their own lives and those of their families by helping Jews. Those who did help lived in fear of betrayal by their neighbours, some of whom hunted Jews in hiding to blackmail them, or to gain a reward from handing them over to the Nazis. One third of the Jews in hiding died.

About 200,000 Jews survived the Holocaust in hiding. Every one of them needed help from their non-Jewish neighbours: a place to hide, someone to bring them food and water, to remove their waste, to provide false documents. Here you can see the identity card of Rosa Buchtal, stamped with a 'J' to show that she is Jewish, and next to it her false 'Aryan' papers provided by the Dutch resistance.

I have always maintained we do not hold it against anyone who did not assist or did not help for reasons that are understandable. It was the death penalty for them and for their families for aiding and abetting Jews. We don't hold it against these people and we are eternally grateful to those who did help, you can never be grateful enough and no matter what you do it is never enough. Those who pointed at you and those who denounced you for no reason – that is the horror of it ...

Lili Pohlmann

Some historians have said that those who didn't save Jews are partly responsible for the Holocaust.

• Do you think that this accusation is fair?

Henri Obstfeld

Henri Obstfeld was just two years old when he was placed in hiding. Dutch couple Jacob and Hendrika Klerk, who told their neighbours that his parents had been killed in the bombing of Rotterdam, sheltered Henri in their home. All he brought with him was one blanket and a teddy bear.

Henri's parents were also in hiding. They didn't see their son for nearly four years. During this time, Henri's father made storybooks and had them smuggled to his son. All survived, and Henri was finally reunited with his parents at the end of the war, when he was five years old.

Georgy Halpern

In 1938, when Austria united with Hitler's Germany, the Halpern family left their home to escape the Nazis and sought refuge in France. But just two years later Germany invaded France.

The French authorities rounded up 'foreign Jews' and imprisoned them in internment camps, later deporting thousands to the death camps in Poland. The Halperns placed their only son, Georgy, in an orphanage that hid Jewish children.

Georgy and his parents were able to write to each other and, although he missed them very much, Georgy was very happy in the orphanage. He enjoyed going for hikes in the mountains around the village and loved playing with the other children.

This is a letter that Georgy wrote to his father. He signed off with 'millions of kisses' and drew a bunch of flowers, 'for mummy'. It was to be the last letter they ever had from him. The Nazi secret police – the *Gestapo* – discovered that the orphanage was hiding Jewish children. They raided the orphanage and sent the children and their teachers to Auschwitz, where Georgy was murdered in the gas chambers.

He was just eight years old.

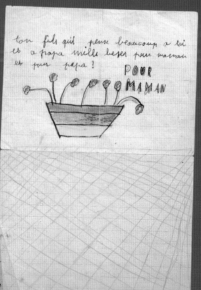

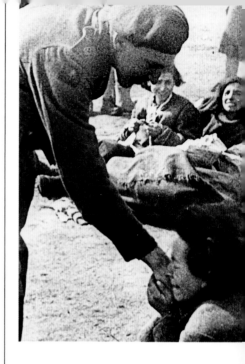

*I remember during that march ... seeing little houses ...
red-roofed, pretty little houses ... and curtains, windows,
lace-curtained windows, and people peering out, staring.
And I often wondered what went on in their minds when
they saw these so-called people being marched in their
concentration camp garb ... I remember thinking ...
a world like that exists? There is another world ...*

Esther Brunstein

By 1944 the defeat of Nazi Germany was certain, but still the
Nazis were determined to murder as many Jews as possible.
Rather than leaving the last camp survivors behind as they
retreated from Eastern Europe, the Nazis forced these
starving people to walk hundreds of miles on 'death marches'
towards Germany. Thousands died from exhaustion and cold
on the way, or were shot on the roadside where they fell.

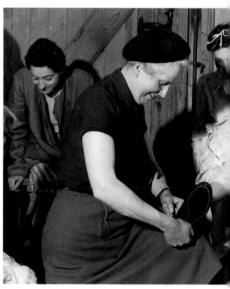

*Those who were nursed back to
health now had to begin a new life.
They were given clothes; children
were given schooling; but how could
life ever return to normal? For most
of those who left the camps, nothing
of their previous lives remained.
Their friends and families were dead.*

Painting by Jan Hartman.

*Jan Hartman was force-marched from Auschwitz to Bielsko in Southwest
Poland. His shoes were too small, the weather was freezing, and he had
been beaten so badly that his back was bent, but he managed to keep
walking along a road lined with the corpses of fallen prisoners. From
Bielsko he and his brother were taken in open wagons to Buchenwald,
a concentration camp inside Germany.*

Discovery and rehabilitation

In the closing months of the war in Europe, Allied soldiers of Britain, the United States and the Soviet Union discovered concentration camps crammed with tens of thousands of the dead and the dying.

This scene of 'liberation' at Bergen-Belsen has become the lasting image of the Holocaust for many British people: the moment when a British soldier is thanked by one of the few survivors of the Holocaust. It is an image of rescue that seemed to justify the long years of hardship that Britain had endured in fighting the Second World War. But should this be our lasting memory of the Holocaust? Could the Allies have done more to save the Jews of Europe?

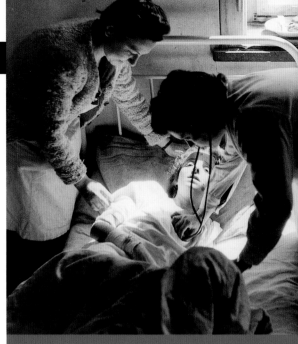

Medical teams gave whatever help they could, but thousands continued to die.

Some of those who had survived the Holocaust returned home only to be murdered by local antisemites when they reached their old home town. Hundreds of thousands decided to leave Europe forever, to go to Palestine and rebuild a Jewish homeland so that they would never again be a persecuted minority.

Compare this photograph with the picture of the British soldier entering Bergen-Belsen (top left). Taken in 1946, we see Jews still in the same camp a year later, now protesting about British policies that prevented them from going to Palestine, which remained under British control. Thousands who were caught trying to enter Palestine illegally again found themselves behind barbed wire, this time in British camps in Cyprus. It was not until 1948, and the foundation of the state of Israel, that the last survivors finally left the Displaced Persons camps.

Hannah Sachsel

Hannah Sachsel and her sister Eva were two of the 60,000 starving people the British found when they entered the German concentration camp of Bergen-Belsen. Hannah drew this picture from her hospital bed, a scene that shows the care she and her sister were given. But for many this care came too late. Shortly after she drew this picture, Hannah died in hospital, hundreds of miles from her home in Czechoslovakia.

She was fourteen years old.

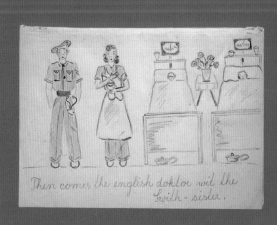

A former prisoner accuses a concentration camp guard

At the end of the war a few people suddenly found themselves in positions of power over those who had persecuted them.

The Nuremberg trial defendants in court

In the siding there were two or three trainloads of Germans ... prisoners who were taken to Russia. I started speaking to one of the Russian soldiers there and explained who I was and so on and so he said, 'If you want to kill a few I'll give you my machine gun and get a few out.' So I said, 'I'm sorry I'm not going to stoop to that.' And I didn't do it of course.

Henry Abisch

We stayed in stables and there was a German officer hiding there. We found him and we did exactly the same as they did to us, we tied him to a tree and we shot him. If you said to me now to do it, no way could I, but at that time it was sweet; I enjoyed it.

Szmulek Gontarz

How could there ever be justice for the murder of a whole people? What punishment could possibly fit such a crime? These are the questions that faced the world.

- Should all Germans have been punished for the Holocaust?
- How would it be possible not to punish the innocent along with the guilty?

Some Allied soldiers who discovered the camps were so angry at what they found that they made the local German population, including children as young as three years old, look into open pits full of naked corpses.

- Was this justice, or vengeance?

The most senior Nazis were put on trial in Nuremberg in 1945. Thousands of lower ranking Nazis were tried over the next few years. Some of those convicted were executed.

Most received prison sentences but many were released after only a few years. The majority of those responsible for the Holocaust were never brought to trial at all.

Some of those directly involved in the Holocaust assumed false identities or fled abroad at the end of the war. A few still live among us today.

- Should these old men be found and brought to trial, or did their crimes happen too long ago?

For the few survivors of the Holocaust who are still alive, their pain and suffering continues to this day.

Once tortured, somehow you always remain tortured for the rest of your life, and you're never quite at ease with human kind. And it has been true for me for a very, very long time.

Esther Brunstein

Never again?

The cry of 'Never again!' has a hollow ring to it. There have been too many genocides before and since the Holocaust for this slogan to have real meaning.

Native Americans, Australian Aborigines, African victims of the slave trade: all have been murdered in their millions. In modern times, the rulers of the Turkish empire murdered one million Armenians. Almost two million people were killed in Cambodia and one million Tutsis were murdered by Hutus in Rwanda. 'Ethnic cleansing' in Bosnia saw Christian Serbs murdering their Muslim neighbours and forcing them into concentration camps. Tens of thousands of Albanians were murdered in Kosovo in your lifetime.

And suffering is not confined only to mass murder. Racism and prejudice exist everywhere, including the town in which you live. More people have died from hunger and disease than have been killed in genocides. Most of the people of the world live in hunger while a minority have too much to eat. The environment is destroyed by pollution we all help to create.

You can make a difference by the way you choose to live your life. But if you do nothing, you cannot pretend that you are unaware of what is happening.

> *There is no excuse for you – for it is your duty to know and to be haunted by your knowledge.*
>
> Arthur Koestler